30 day poet

feed your writer's bug

Mia White

Dedicated to:

My indescribably beautiful, word-artist
friend and editor;

Mahreen Shamim.

Begging heaven for creative ideas,
you became mine.

CONTENTS

ACKNOWLEDGMENTS

My abundant gratitude goes to the Source of all beautiful creativity. You, who make me come alive.

INTRODUCTION

I groaned with inward envy as I read my friend's Facebook post. She was entering a Thirty Day Novel Writing Contest. In my imagination of another time, another place and another life, I instantly saw myself in an oversized sweater. (Like the one that big uncle left behind after the Christmas party and you rescued from the give-away bag.) There is a giant coffee pot by my side and crumbled balls of paper all around. One single lamp is lit. It's not too bright and not too dark. There's just enough of a spotlight to create a bubble of warmth around me in a dusky room. There is fire in my eyes and my fingers are racing over the keyboard. Wait, no, the typewriter. Tap, tap, tap. . .Tap, tap, tap. . .Yup, that's my one year old hitting the spoon of porridge on her head.

In reality, I'm a mother of eight kids and not a novel writer at all. There is no time. There are a million odd socks and thousands of dishes calling for me even when the brood doesn't. So, I groan inwardly, sigh and feel sorry for myself, . . .even though I normally like my life. I think it's because there's a writer's bug who lives inside of me that needs to be fed. He is very hungry, and when he starves he literally starts eating me.

So. . .a few days later (after the groaning spurred on by Facebook), I'm in a park, hosting a birthday fall picnic for small humans. And I have this idea. Like a defiant stubborn voice on the inside kind of idea. I'm gonna make my own challenge. I'm gonna write every day for a whole month, too. Like all these other unobstructed adult people. Yes, I am. I may not have time to write a novel, but I'm gonna write. . .(O God what am I gonna write?!)I'm gonna write. . .poetry! Poetry can be short. Yes it can. I'm going to be a freaking 30 day poet!

So, here is my first poem, from that very moment in time, walking over an autumn field in the park (far away from frolicking little ones since I had visited the bathroom alone for a change). And this is a bonus one. . .aside from the thirty. . . just because:

Those are my footsteps
Echoing behind me

I'm the only one around
The ruffle in the leaves
Are made by me

I must be alive
After all

That's it. I did it. I started. Poem number one. Check. I didn't have to pull my hair, rub my temples, or pace back and forth. It didn't only come easy, it felt great, in all its simplicity and briefness.

Throughout my self-imposed challenge I discovered much. I discovered that sometimes an experience or sentiment or even a memory doesn't come "into itself" until it's put into words. Like a movie needs a music score to set the mood, so life needs words to make it poetic. I discovered that within me were things sad, tragic, depressing, deep, defiant, frightening, sarcastic, happy, funny, hilarious and beautiful that wanted. . .no, *craved*, words.

I share my 30 day poems with you in this book, with the purpose of encouraging you to add poetic scores to your own life. Because if you don't, many things may be misjudged and never come into themselves. Parts of your story that may have seemed ordinary to you may turn out to be quite astonishing. Thoughts and sentiments that are familiar companions to you may actually be quite radical. What may have the appearance of comfortable contentment on the inside of you may actually disguise itself as slumbering creative frustration. I suspect that deep down there are incubated treasures longing to be unearthed and discovered. Who knows, perhaps like me, you may even find a very hungry writer's bug within.

Speaking of which, all throughout this book you will find these little endearing bugs that are carrying inspirational ideas your way. You may want to use them if you feel writer's block setting in on occasion, as you begin your own 30 day poetry challenge. This journal also includes a word bank with plenty of cha-ching ideas in the back of the book and some "poetry starters" to use, under dire circumstances, if need be.

I have made sure to leave plenty of space for you to brainstorm, mind-map, doodle, jot and create in the following pages to unlock your inner Poe (short for Poet but hilariously also one of the best known POEts in America; Edgar Allan Poe).

May this book become your best friend and most trusted confidant for *at least* 30 days (and then a treasured possession for life, containing a part of you). And may it help you discover (as it did for me) that you are truly alive. . .After all.

Are we all bewilderedly observing
Life's peculiar foreign
Happenstance

Wondering if we are the only one
Not knowing the steps
To this dance

- created a queen { pic of running to Dad

- killing the children
  - all children under 2 yo (Jesus)
  - lies of the enemy about Dad-Chuck

- tormentors
  - chuck
  - bullies @ school

- Being Different
  - I was an outsider (didn't fit in)

DOODELING & BRAIN-STORMING

1. commoners becoming royalty — stuff of fairy tales

Not to bug you or anything, but if you need an idea before I bugger off: Why not look around you where you are right now and write a poem about what you see. It can be about the room, the environment, the context, the people, or the atmosphere.

ROUGH DRAFT

POEM 1

DAY 2

My eyes crave color
Like my lungs crave air
Contrasts and pallets
In the richest of fare

A passionfruit cut open
Orange purple red
A sunset by the ocean
Pink and firebred

The iris of an eye
In all the shades of brown
A cardinal in flight
In its crimson shimmering gown

The tops of chains of mountains
In glistening icy white
Storm clouds on the horizon
Let the grays display their might

A field of tulips at spring time
A forest vibrant at fall
My eyes can't even contain that breath
And the ecstasy of it all

DOODELING & BRAIN-STORMING

Not to bug you or anything, but if you need an idea before I bugger off: Brainstorm about who you are and start your poem with "I am. . .".

ROUGH DRAFT

POEM 2

_____

_____

_____

_____

_____

_____

_____

_____

_____

_____

_____

_____

_____

_____

_____

_____

_____

_____

_____

_____

_____

_____

_____

_____

DAY 3

Depression is not your forever
It only pretends to be

It lacks enduring properties
Like a mere leaf on a tree

When it falls
And it will
There are root-like things
Deeper still

Push-through-hopeful-things
That always will

Remain
Your evergreen

DOODELING & BRAIN-STORMING

Not to bug you or anything, but if you need an idea before I bugger off: Why not write a poem using the words 'Ground', 'Fly' and 'Clouds'?

ROUGH DRAFT

POEM 3

POETRY POINTER #1

In poetry as in life: *Less words are often more*.

The goal is to create strong visual imagery

with few words.

Be brutal in your word chopping.

Comb away all the unnecessary,

so that what is left will have more oomph.

DAY 4

Like withered muscles
Are the spirits of men

When one is alive
I look again

If it wasn't for the statue
Concealed in the stone

The army would be lost
In the valley of bones

DOODELING & BRAIN-STORMING

Not to bug you or anything, but if you
need an idea before I bugger off:
Why not write a poem using opposites
(Black-white, hot-cold, light-dark. . .)?

ROUGH DRAFT

POEM 4

DAY 5

The path
Of least resistance

Has completely
Altered maps

DOODELING & BRAIN-STORMING

Not to bug you or anything, but if you need an idea before I bugger off: Write a poem about the state of the world (such as famine, war, injustice. . .).

ROUGH DRAFT

POEM 5

DAY 6

Some people
May think
I've lost my way

At the exact time
I'm finally
Starting to find it

DOODELING & BRAIN-STORMING

Not to bug you or anything, but if you need an idea before I bugger off: List several words describing how you feel right now. Use your adjectives to create a poem.

ROUGH DRAFT

POEM 6

POETRY POINTER #2

To rhyme, or not to rhyme?
Why not! But do try both.
If you do however, be extra careful to find
and follow a **pattern**.

As you divide the poem into lines and sections,
make sure that the rhymes come in
the same place each time;
for example, at the end of every other line.

The goal is for the reader to find
the **flow** that you intended.

DAY 7

If a heart was just a thing
It wouldn't matter

You can break my vase
Lose my keys
Ignore my message
Step on my shoes

But my heart–

What will it do
Without wings

DOODELING & BRAIN-STORMING

Not to bug you or anything, but if you
need an idea before I bugger off:
Pick out three words from the word bank
in the back of the book and use them in
your poem.

ROUGH DRAFT

POEM 7

_____

_____

_____

_____

_____

_____

_____

_____

_____

_____

_____

_____

_____

_____

_____

_____

_____

_____

_____

_____

_____

_____

DAY 8

She lived to be a hundred and three
And used rubbing alcohol for every remedy

Baked pound cake and drank lots of tea
And always had enough change for a treat

She read her Bible with huge letters to see
And sat in her chair re-living each memory

Never complained about the things that be
Didn't judge even when she didn't agree

Light as a feather with roots like a tree
I long to live as free as she

DOODELING & BRAIN-STORMING

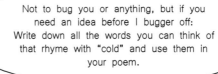

Not to bug you or anything, but if you
need an idea before I bugger off:
Write down all the words you can think of
that rhyme with "cold" and use them in
your poem.

ROUGH DRAFT

POEM 8

DAY 9

You know that beetle
With the huge claws

It gives me chills
It's so beautiful

If I met one
I would run in terror

And then wish
I could see it again

Oh to be
Dangerously
Ferociously
Intriguingly
Terrifyingly
Beautiful

DOODELING & BRAIN-STORMING

Not to bug you or anything, but if you need an idea before I bugger off: Write a poem about your closest relationship.

ROUGH DRAFT

POEM 9

DAY 10

Today was the first time
You scraped your hands
Falling on the concrete

So happy running
And then

You met life
And it met you
H-a-r-d

It wasn't a major event
So why did make me gasp

Perhaps it was a reminder
The life I birthed you into
Will one day scrape your heart

DOODELING & BRAIN-STORMING

Not to bug you or anything, but if you
need an idea before I bugger off:
Write down as many synonyms to "road"
that you can think of, and use them to
write a poem.

ROUGH DRAFT

POEM 10

po•et

ˈpōət

noun

noun: **poet**;
plural noun: **poets**

a person who writes poems.

Synonyms: writer of poetry, versifier, rhymester, rhymer, sonneteer, lyricist, lyrist;

- o a person possessing special powers of imagination or expression.[i]

po•em

'pōəm,pōm

noun

noun: **poem**;
plural noun: **poems**

a piece of writing that partakes of the nature of both speech and song that is nearly always rhythmical, usually metaphorical, and often exhibits such formal elements as meter, rhyme, and stanzaic structure.

Synonyms: verse, rhyme, piece of poetry, song

"Lydia saved every poem that Marshall wrote that year"

o something that arouses strong emotions because of its beauty.

"you make a poem of riding downhill on your bike"[ii]

DAY 11

There's a sign hanging on my door
Not accepting suitors anymore
You didn't see that sign you say
Well it shouldn't matter anyway
Surely you can read it on my face

DOODELING & BRAIN-STORMING

Not to bug you or anything, but if you
need an idea before I bugger off:
Write a poem about your favorite
season. Use all your senses: what does
the season smell, taste, look, feel and
sound like. . .

ROUGH DRAFT

POEM 11

DAY 12

We should write a book about that day
As the rarest of events
When we all felt content
At the same time

There is always a fire over here
Or a fight over there

A heart that needs to heal
A bruised elbow, a scraped knee

A runny nose to wipe
A water hose that ran all night

Keys misplaced
Shoes that can't be laced

A relationship gone sour
Late for school a whole hour

Bills that can't be paid
Someone who's afraid

A long sleepless night
Wishing for a kite

Food too hot, food gone cold
That thing on e-bay that won't be sold

Missing that other place
Longing for a new phase

That book calling from the shelf
Always someone needing help

It's absurd really
But then again
We are
A family of TEN.

DOODELING & BRAIN-STORMING

Not to bug you or anything, but if you
need an idea before I bugger off:
Start a poem with these words: "The
never-ending saga. . .".

ROUGH DRAFT

POEM 12

DAY 13

Then it dawned on me
If no one reads a single word I write
Like a midnight forest shout
When no one is around
It still matters.

Every word echoes
Between my inner mountains and hills
Sending ripples into the world through me
And trees do hear
Don't they?

DOODELING & BRAIN-STORMING

Not to bug you or anything, but if you need
an idea before I bugger off:
Choose one adjective, one verb and one
noun from the word bank and use them in
a poem.

ROUGH DRAFT

POEM 13

_____

_____

_____

_____

_____

_____

_____

_____

_____

_____

_____

_____

_____

_____

_____

_____

_____

_____

_____

_____

_____

_____

_____

_____

POETRY POINTER #3

Adjectives are your most precious tool
in coloring a poem.

Make use of the internet to find
exciting **synonyms** for what you want to describe.

Try to stay away from common expressions.
Find an **original** way to express
even familiar concepts.

DAY 14

Guess what
I choose you
You over there
To be my friend

You with the scarred-up face
So frail and feeble
With pin-marked arms
From too many needles

I choose you
Rubbed raw
Beaten blue
Without your due
Being given to you

But will you have me
Hesitant one
I'm really kind
Please don't run

Or did you detect
Driving this cause
My very own need
To be Santa Claus

DOODELING & BRAIN-STORMING

Not to bug you or anything, but if you need an idea before I bugger off: Choose two words out of the letter K-section in the word-bank and create a poem around them.

ROUGH DRAFT

POEM 14

DAY 15

I have three lofty goals in life

To give
To serve
To lift up

So if I give nothing
If I fail to serve
If I ever push you down

It's only because
I've temporarily
Ran aground

DOODELING & BRAIN-STORMING

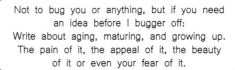

Not to bug you or anything, but if you need
an idea before I bugger off:
Write about aging, maturing, and growing up.
The pain of it, the appeal of it, the beauty
of it or even your fear of it.

ROUGH DRAFT

POEM 15

DAY 16

Hollywood
Hail the hollow

Hollywood
Hail the hoax

Hollywood
Hail the hypocrisy

Isn't it hilarious
That we hunt for our heroes

In this hiding-place
Of such homeless hearts

DOODELING & BRAIN-STORMING

Not to bug you or anything, but if you need
an idea before I bugger off:
Write about when you were a child. Jot
down words and short phrases that describe
your childhood and use them in your poem.

ROUGH DRAFT

POEM 16

POETRY POINTER #4

Poetry benefits from **rhythm**
even though it doesn't have music.
To help find the "beat" of your creation
you can decide on an amount of
syllables in each line
and stick to it.

If you feel like coloring outside the lines
of this principle that's ok too,
just don't vary the syllable amount
too much from line to line.

It's all about the **flow** of the reading experience
and effect it will have.

DAY 17

Incompetent
Insignificant
Insecure
Insufficient
Inhibited
Incomplete

Considering how these words
Limit, maim, and fence people in
If life had a dictionary
I would render them obsolete

DOODELING & BRAIN-STORMING

Not to bug you or anything, but if you need
an idea before I bugger off:
Write a poem about hope.

ROUGH DRAFT

POEM 17

DAY 18

The road less travelled
The song less sung
Being humble and wise
While still being young

DOODELING & BRAIN-STORMING

Not to bug you or anything, but if you
need an idea before I bugger off:
Think about a person in your life and
write a poem about them, as if you
were them.

ROUGH DRAFT

POEM 18

DAY 19

My hands are tied by love
As you wander
I bite my tongue in love
I foresee your blunder

My hands can't protect you
Any longer
I fold them and pray
That you heal stronger

My words can't restrain you
      Anymore
I use them to declare
My ceiling will be your floor

DOODELING & BRAIN-STORMING

Not to bug you or anything, but if you
need an idea before I bugger off:
Write a poem that alternates between
phrases starting with "You say. . ."
and "I say. . .".

ROUGH DRAFT

POEM 19

DAY 20

If black and white make gray
And blue and red make purple
What will you and I make

DOODELING & BRAIN-STORMING

Not to bug you or anything, but if you need
an idea before I bugger off:
Write a poem about the things that have
stood out this past week of your life.

ROUGH DRAFT

POEM 20

THAT POEt

Edgar Allan Poe (/poʊ/; born Edgar Poe; January 19, 1809 – October 7, 1849) was an American writer, editor, and literary critic. Poe is best known for his poetry and short stories, particularly his tales of mystery and the macabre. He is widely regarded as a central figure of Romanticism in the United States and American literature as a whole, and he was one of the country's earliest practitioners of the short story. Poe is generally considered the inventor of the detective fiction genre and is further credited with contributing to the emerging genre of science fiction.[iii] He was the first well-known American writer to try to earn a living through writing alone, resulting in a financially difficult life and career.[iv] [v]

Just look at this dude! He deserves his place in history just from his priceless face. I am falling in love with the idea of this poor fresh fledgling poet, so beaten up by life, who gave it all for his creative expression. He died when he was my age (unlike him I pray I don't look 20 years older than I am). I mean, the dress code, the hair-do, the extreme plea in his eyes, for someone (just someone!) to take him seriously. I will take you home and listen to your angst over a cup of tea, don't be sad. It will all work out in the end. . .I think.

Here's to you Poe. Another bonus one for the count:

What do you see
In my posing face
Stoic confidence
Or a cry for grace
Do you detect the bags
Under my piercing eyes
Can you see
That they are trained for lies
Do you read the despair
On my brow between the lines
Have you seen it before
In artists of all kinds
If only someone could make
That inward roaring beast be tame
But then again
No one would ever know my name

. . .And here's one of Mr. Poe's famous poems called *"A Dream Within a Dream"* (published 1849). Perhaps, after reading it, you will thank me for not being as deep as he is; honestly, sometimes this guy loses me. But I love his stamina in being intensely dramatic in all he writes. It certainly worked for his time. Perhaps you are the "Poe" of today, with a new creative way to say what your hearts wants to convey.

Take this kiss upon the brow!
And, in parting from you now,
Thus much let me avow —
You are not wrong, who deem
That my days have been a dream;
Yet if hope has flown away
In a night, or in a day,
In a vision, or in none,
Is it therefore the less gone?
All that we see or seem
Is but a dream within a dream.

I stand amid the roar
Of a surf-tormented shore,
And I hold within my hand
Grains of the golden sand —
How few! yet how they creep
Through my fingers to the deep,
While I weep — while I weep!
O God! Can I not grasp
Them with a tighter clasp?
O God! can I not save
One from the pitiless wave?
Is all that we see or seem
But a dream within a dream?

DAY 21

What shall we do
About all the love
That will never change
The world

There is so much of it
I'm not sure
Any more
Can fit

Love that asks your
Phase or faith
Color or race
Skill or pace

Love that checks the
Thrill of the chase
Strength of the blaze
Satin and lace

What shall we do
About the lack
Of love
That remains

DOODELING & BRAIN-STORMING

Not to bug you or anything, but if you
need an idea before I bugger off:
Write a poem about politics, politicians or
a hot political issue.

ROUGH DRAFT

POEM 21

DAY 22

I'm not afraid of your demons
I can see right through them
I see what's true
I see you

DOODELING & BRAIN-STORMING

Not to bug you or anything, but if you
need an idea before I bugger off:
Choose five words from the second half of
the word bank in the back of the book and
use them in your poem.

ROUGH DRAFT

POEM 22

DAY 23

What's the ulterior motive
For being so kind

What piece of your puzzle
Did you think you finally found

I hate to burst that bubble
You so skillfully blow

But I'm an entire puzzle
All on my very own

DOODELING & BRAIN-STORMING

Not to bug you or anything, but if you need
an idea before I bugger off:
Write a poem on the common theme of
Love. Try not to use familiar concepts.

ROUGH DRAFT

POEM 23

POETRY POINTER #5

The **last line** of your poems will be
the most crucial one.
Spend extra time mulling it over.
Consider different options
to find the one with the most effect.

An **element of surprise** at the end
is just as powerful as the unexpected twist
at the end a movie or book.
You want to leave your reader with a
powerful last punch and make them
gasp with emotion.

DAY 24

Give me just one flower
The smallest of its kind
Let me study it one hour
It will smooth my brow and mind

Give me just one flower
Let it sing to me its psalm
The life-blood of creation
My elixir of healing balm

DOODELING & BRAIN-STORMING

Not to bug you or anything, but if you
need an idea before I bugger off:
Write a poem using the theme of water.

ROUGH DRAFT

POEM 24

DAY 25

Surely my friend
It must be easier to find yourself
When you're not searching
In a crowd

DOODELING & BRAIN-STORMING

Not to bug you or anything, but if you
need an idea before I bugger off:
Use the word "Up" in each line of your
poem. (Think growing up, stepping up,
looking up etc.)

ROUGH DRAFT

POEM 25

DAY 26

If no two are alike
Then let no two be alike

Further Fashion Freedom
And Totally Truthful Transparency

Plain is as Pretty
As Extravagant is Extra

So let us Be the Billboards
Of all the Benchmarks we have Braved

DOODELING & BRAIN-STORMING

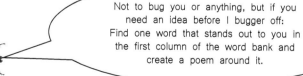

Not to bug you or anything, but if you
need an idea before I bugger off:
Find one word that stands out to you in
the first column of the word bank and
create a poem around it.

ROUGH DRAFT

POEM 26

POETRY POINTER #6

Don't be afraid to let a family member
or close friend read your poetry
and give **feed back**.

Chances are, if there are things they don't get,
or places where they can't find
the flow you intended,
other readers might not either.

Unless your poetry is for your own eyes only,
be willing to receive **constructive criticism**.

DAY 27

As I microwave my coffee for the fourth time
With my head wrapped in plastic over hair dye this time
I decide that somehow this is a poetic moment
I suspect that others have more orderly lives
That they can sit down at mealtime and lie down at
bedtime
Drink their coffee while its hot
And not change their hair color while cooking
But I decide – In This Moment – to love my life
And my eight children
And the dishes competing with the laundry mountain
And the jelly stains on the mat
And the Legos on the floor
And the crust under the sofa
And the one–sock–one–shoe drama
And every DVD and cd being scratched
And the toothpaste on the mirror
And the throw up on my shoulder
And the snot stains on my pant legs
And the short times of sleep
And the shorter times of rest
To me my life is poetry
At least when I decide to make it so
Oh...my coffee!

DOODELING & BRAIN-STORMING

Not to bug you or anything, but if you need
an idea before I bugger off:
Think of a painful memory from your life and
go all out. Be dramatic. Pour out your guts.
If you like, you can still end the poem on a
hopeful note.

ROUGH DRAFT

POEM 27

DAY 28

Don't know what else to do
I surrender to the devouring

Go ahead pain have your feast
Hopefully at the end of it

Though the "self" in myself will be gone
The "my" still remains

As the bones in a carcass
To hold the new man

DOODELING & BRAIN-STORMING

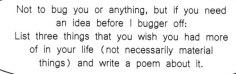

Not to bug you or anything, but if you need
an idea before I bugger off:
List three things that you wish you had more
of in your life (not necessarily material
things) and write a poem about it.

ROUGH DRAFT

POEM 28

DAY 29

I would if I could protect you
Little Red Riding Hood
Basket full of goodies
Skipping into a darkened wood

Humming a jovial melody
Then eye to eye with the beast
How did you endure the devouring
As your purity turned his feast

I would if I could convince you
That the end of the story is great
The huntsman in the forest
Is the one who holds your fate

DOODELING & BRAIN-STORMING

Not to bug you or anything, but if you need
an idea before I bugger off:
Write a poem about breaking patterns or
habits in your life.

ROUGH DRAFT

POEM 29

DAY 30

I want shoes with signs of travel
Color worn off
Soles loose
Knotted shoestrings never to be untied

I want hands with callouses and rough spots
Knees with scars and memories
I want skin with freckles and red cheeks
From its share of sun and chilly breeze

And when I am old and tired
And sit in my comfortable chair
Dreaming of the adventures that I've had
Reminiscing smiling chuckling

Collected in my mind
Will be my loved ones, each one
And on the mantel piece right in front of me
Instead of pictures in frames

I will put the shoes that carried me far
The spade that helped me plant my seeds
The feathers I dropped learning to fly
And a bottle with all the tears I cried

And lastly
My book of poetry
My music score to life

DOODELING & BRAIN-STORMING

Not to bug you or anything, but if you
need an idea before I bugger off: Write a
poem about how you experience writing.

ROUGH DRAFT

POEM 30

Welcome across the finish-line my friend. How does it feel? Was it a steep climb? A downward slope? Or a level plain?. . .a level desert plain perhaps?. . .or a level ice-rink on wobbly skates? If you are like me, spouting out poetic rhythm and rhyme has become like a bug I caught. (No wonder, this book is full of them). I can't get rid of it now. What you can't beat, join. I truly feel a taste for more and hope you do too.

I also hope you feel a surprising pat on your back from. . .oh yourself! That satisfaction from the revelation that you did it. And now I extend the invitation for you to share your greatness with others so that they can praise you too. . .if they are able to see your brilliance, and if you want them to. You can find the *30 Day Poet* page on Facebook and post your favorite creation from this month there if you like. (Only one please, and your name is optional. Just don't use someone else's. . .poem or name.) I would be delighted and so honored to read it.

Also, if you feel like continuing to challenge yourself and spread the love, why not get a group of friends together and order the **Poetry Workbook for Individuals and Groups:** *"Feed Your Writer's Bug"*. Doesn't writing together, reading your creations to each other and ending your 10 weeks with a great poetry slam sounds both stretching, liberating and rewarding?! (Why not couple the poetry night with fundraising for a great cause, and perhaps invite a local writer to share the stage with you?! Your options are limitless.)

And now, as we are comrades in the Living Poets Society:

I lift my quill in the air,
Bow low with dramatic flair
Release my last words like a bell
Most courageous fellow Poe
Farewell.

WORD-BANK FULL OF RICHES

Adaptable	Calibrated	Fringe	Host
Anthem	Callous	Feel	Hotel
Anxious	Circus	Flood	Hungry
Antidote	Caffeine	Flag	Healthy
Ambitious	Cunning	Find	Hounding
Africa	Centipede	Frown	Injured
Altogether	Century	Functional	Icy
Albeit	Dreamy	Financial	Idyllic
Albatross	Develop	Faceless	Intrigued
Abiding	Delving	Friendly	Infatuated
Airplane	Diving	Feign	Intifada
Airborne	Dainty	Fabricated	India
Aphrodisiac	Damned	Feign	Indigo
Arbitrary	Diversity	Freedom	Ignitable
Angry	Dread	Front	Illusional
Angelic	Dreary	Green	Ill
Abloom	Diary	Grown	Illustrated
Beauty	Dire	Grant	Illustrious
Backstage	Devious	Galore	Infiltration
Beatitude	Drug	Gaping	Ink
Benchmark	Drunk	Grill	Incomplete
Belittle	Dapper	Grunt	Incoming
Breakable	Dazed	Gray	Jump
Backward	Decimal	Genetic	Jesus
Bacterial	Dog	Gigantic	Jazzy
Bestow	Dig	Gazelle	Jovial
Beast	Daffodil	Ghastly	Jostle
Brink	Drumbeat	Giving	Jest
Brute	Dusty	Graying	Jog
Binge	Effortless	Getable	Jeans
Benevolent	Eastward	Grazing	Janitor
Biased	Earthy	Galloping	Jungle
Bellow	Echoless	Gone	Jingle
Culprit	Enter	Home	Jug
Center	Entourage	Hell	Junk
Centered	Endearing	Habitual	Jasper
Central	Educated	Hunt	Kilter
Corny	Endless	Hound	Keen
Cadent	Enemy	Hint	Kindred
Cancerous	Energy	Hammered	Kill
Chance	Energetic	Hardcover	Knightly
Chanel	Engaging	Hollow	Ken
Chronic	Elope	Hilarious	Knobbly
Chastise	Ebony	Hazel	Kosher
Chaste	Fleeting	Hanging	Knowable
Castle	Frightened	Haste	Knitted

Kernel	Note	Rose	Uniform
Klondike	Ninja	Rift	Unicorn
Kettled	Nonsense	Riff raff	Unction
Kindle	Number	Role	Umbrella
Kia	Neon	Rust	Understanding
Kitten	Never	Risk	Uber
Kinkade	No	Robust	Underbite
King	Numb	Rio	USA
Kingdom	Oval	Ruffled	Unity
Lemons	Over	Roaring	Unify
Level	Onsite	Reeling	University
Lavender	Onset	Ringing	Varsity
Labeled	Omniscient	Rotting	Vanity
Labored	Omega	Rude	Vintage
Lavish	Ongoing	Rogue	Vinery
Lint	Orange	Sting	Vineyard
Lustrous	Orient	Stout	Vent
Lacking	Omniscient	Serene	Vortex
Lame	Often	Strung	Violet
Lamented	Older	Strength	Victorious
Lawful	Openness	Sturdy	Violin
Lump	Opener	Sift	Vault
Longing	Priestly	Soft	Vienna
Lodge	Poignant	Slimy	Varied
Ledge	Piercing	Staff	Variables
Load	Pink	Stall	Veritable
Lofty	Pest	Sung	Vegetarian
Lengthy	Pet	Song	Wow
Loving	Prudent	Serenade	Wing
Lethal	Pontify	Soil	Wand
Mostly	Pope	Strip	Want
Memory	Pray	Stop	Why
Militant	Plead	Snap	Winged
Moth	Please	Sinister	Wilt
Mold	Plow	Trump	Wondering
Mend	Plight	Triumph	Wick
Master	Puppy	Trample	Welter
Mister	Quest	Triangle	Wild
Muster	Question	Taunt	Wilderness
Mindful	Queen	Trite	Wrought
Minister	Quackery	Tamper	Wronged
Mess	Quick	Tower	Yo-yo
Macabre	Quake	Tinker	Yonder
Nose	Quaking	Tall	Yesterday
Nice	Qualify	Trust	Young
Notorious	Quality	Tide	Yes
Neat	Quantity	Thousand	Zest
Nesting	Rant	Thrift	Zoom
Net	Rest	Underdog	Zeal

LIST OF POEM-STARTERS

1. I never thought I would dive so deep. . .
2. From hence forth. . .
3. Velvety, silky and soft. . .
4. The furthest distance. . .
5. You can climb a ladder. . .
6. Like the wind and trickling water. . .
7. I see your dreamy gaze and wonder. . .
8. Brick by brick. . .
9. Patience is not my strength. . .
10. I melted like wax before the flame. . .
11. Only in the eyes of a child. . .
12. I thought if I could stay on top. . .
13. Are more words really necessary. . .
14. What have we done to the planet. . .
15. If I was God. . .
16. What is that peculiar empty shape. . .
17. The distance between hearts and minds. . .
18. Floating on the sea of forgetfulness. . .
19. The never-ending saga. . .
20. The sign said Open. . .
21. I have lost the batteries to my remote. . .
22. Once upon a time. . .
23. It was the best of tries. . .
24. In the dead of night. . .
25. Oh, how I crave perfection. . .
26. What do you see when you look at me. . .
27. There is a kind of friendship. . .
28. Is it all futility and vanity. . .
29. There is joy unspeakable. . .
30. Fleeting are the moments. . .

LOOK OUT FOR THIS TITLE:

**Feed
your writer's bug**

poetry workbook
for individuals and groups

Mia White

[i] Google Dictionary

[ii] Google Dictionary

[iii] **Stableford, Brian** (2003). "Science fiction before the genre". In James, Edward; Mendlesohn, Farah. *The Cambridge Companion to Science Fiction.* Cambridge: Cambridge University Press. pp. 15–31. **ISBN 978-0-521-01657-5**. (sic)

[iv] Meyers, Jeffrey (1992). *Edgar Allan Poe: His Life and Legacy* (Paperback ed.). New York: Cooper Square Press. **ISBN 978-0-8154-1038-6.**

[v] Wikipedia